Taking Back Your Marriage

or

How to Get Your Husband to Fall in Love With You

(Again)

by

Georgia Ivey Green

To my husband and children for their love and support.

Table of Contents

i. Prolog

ii. Introduction

1. About Dominance & Submission

2. What is an FLR?

    1. Why Do You Want An FLR?

    2. Why Does He Want An FLR?

    3. What If He Doesn't Want An FLR?

3. You Have the Power

4. Talk, Talk, Talk

5. Psychology 101

6. Getting Started

7. Methods of Teasing

8. Daily Teasing

    1. While He Is At Work

    2. When He Is At Home

    3. If You Have Kids At Home

9. Tease & Denial

    1. Why Tease?

    2. Why Denial?

3. Handling His Behavior

10. Your First Denial Session

11. Making Your Fantasies Come True

12. What About Chastity?

13. Success Stories

14. How to Approach Your Wife

Prolog

Basic Principles of Controlling a Man

1. A man's libido is what drives him.

- His libido is the driving force behind just about everything he does.

2. A man's fantasies are a direct line to his libido.

- His libido creates fantasies. He has no control over his fantasies.

3. Control his fantasies and you control his libido.

- Put yourself into his fantasies and you can control his libido.

4. A man thinks orgasm is the goal of sex.

- His body has taught him this since puberty.

5. A man will do almost anything to achieve an orgasm.

- Therefore, control his orgasms and you control him.

We will use these five basic principles to guide you through the establishment of a Female lead Relationship in your own home. Notice that none of these principles talk about women or that women are in anyway superior to men. That's because I am NOT a feminist. I do not believe that either gender is superior to the other. I DO believe that each gender is capable of taking control of a family and doing a good job of raising the children and keeping the family safe.

However, I also believe that man are driven by different goals and desires than women. I also believe that many family's would be better served by a female leader. That is why I wrote this book. It is my goal to help those women who feel that their family would be better served if they, themselves, were in control. Women are more family oriented than most men. I also believe that when faced with providing for his family, a man has difficulty in understanding the relationships that effect the families over all well being.

Therefore, there are families who suffer dis-functionality because the roles have not been set up in the ideal manner. Not every home should be female-lead, but there are a great number that would benefit from the leadership of a woman. In these cases, society and its morals and morays often prevents a woman from feeling comfortable taking charge of anything.

The divorce rate in the United States (and other countries) is way too high. It is my belief that if more women would take charge of their men, there would be far fewer divorces. One of the major causes of divorce is "boredom". Men and women alike simply get bored with their marriage and find no other solution to their problems. A female lead relationship, especially in the bedroom, could change all that.

Any woman can do it if she knows how. This book is a guide to help those women take charge of their respective husbands and create a better, more loving, home for their families. It can be done. I know because I have done it and I know many other women (and men) who are much happier since they have switched to a female lead relationship. You can do it, too.

Introduction

Ask yourself, "What would it be like if my husband was more romantic?" Life would be a bit more bearable, perhaps. But what if he were more attentive? Or more help around the house? Would that sound like something that might make your life, especially with him, better? Of course it would. In fact, the main reason anyone (male or female) has an extra-marital affair is because someone, other than their spouse, has been more attentive, more romantic, or even just more attractive, to him/her. Isn't it? Wouldn't it be nice if your husband treated you like "the other woman" in his life? Don't you want to be more attractive to him? If you answered "Yes" to that question, then why not be that other woman?

This book was written for the "average" woman in a "normal" relationship. The woman who wishes her spouse was just a little more attentive, a little more romantic, a little more help around the house, or even a better role model for the kids. I'm not saying that every marriage can be saved simply by applying the things I teach in this book, but if yours is worth saving, why not give it a chance?

This book will teach you how to become that other woman. How to be much more attractive to your husband without dieting or exercising. If you follow the principles I have laid out in this book for you, your husband will not only find you more attractive, he will fall in love with you all over again. And that, my friend, is the purpose of this book. To bring you both closer together and to give you back the love you once felt for each other when you first got married.

You have the power to change, to improve your relationship, in ways you never thought possible. It's called "Erotic Power!" I have done my research, and I can prove that it is far less important to a man what a woman looks like than most people think. Using your erotic power you will be able to prove it to yourself.

Georgia Ivey Green

About Dominance & Submission

There has been a great deal of misconception concerning dominance and submission. Most people think it has something to with BDSM, and at the very least, it means something 'kinky'. To some extent they are correct. But there doesn't have to be anything kinky about it.

Every day you, yourself, are involved in dominance and submission (D/s). In fact, all our lives we are involved in it. As a mother, you may be dominant to your children. As a wife, you may be submissive to your husband. As a working woman, you may be submissive to your boss and dominant to those under you. What I am trying to say is, most of us are dominant in some aspects of our lives while being submissive in others.

So, as you can see, you are already dominant in some ways, you just may not have been aware of it, or thought of it in that way. You may be comfortable being someone's boss at work, but not comfortable being the boss at home. I want to change all that. Just because our society says that when two people get married, the man is supposed to the dominant partner, doesn't mean it always has to be that way. Especially not in our society today. Women now hold much better positions in business than ever before and there is no reason that they cannot be in a position of dominance at home.

That's what this book is about. Taking control of as much (or as little) of your marriage as you would like. It's also about getting what you want and having a husband who is glad to give it to you. You don't have to do anything 'kinky' unless you want to. But that doesn't mean you can sit back and do nothing. You will have to work at it. But no one said it wouldn't require work, just that if you apply the principles taught in this book, you will find it easy and fun.

What if you could improve your marriage? I mean, go back to the way it was when you first got married, or even when you were just dating? Can you remember those days? Wasn't your partner more attentive to your needs? Wasn't he more romantic than he is now? Well, how would like to go back to those days?

Going back in time just isn't feasible. But you can still make things better. Maybe not like they were way back then, maybe even better than they were. It's really all a matter of understanding the way men work. That is, what makes them tick. Once you understand that, and apply a few simple principles to your life, you will see just how easy it is to control your husband and get him to enjoy doing more for you.

Of course, I am talking about your *Erotic Power*. It doesn't matter what you look like. It doesn't matter whether you can still fit into a size two dress (or if you ever could). What matters is that you understand the principles in this book and apply them properly. Honest! It doesn't matter.

Your *Erotic Power* is what makes all things possible. It can turn your husband into the loving, romantic he once was. It can get him to do things you never thought he would do. Why? Because he will want to do them for you. That's right. He will want to do them for you. The fact is, he wants you to be dominant over him. He just may not know it, yet. In fact, he may know it, but you don't. So let's get started. I'll explain everything in the chapters to come. So read on...

What is an FLR?

Just what is a Female Lead Relationship (FLR)? It's just what it sounds like. It's a marriage in which the woman makes most of the decisions. Really, it's that simple! So the real question is, who needs an FLR? Some woman are perfectly happy letting their husband run the show. And that's fine. But if there is anything about your marriage that you would like to improve, perhaps you should take control of, at least, some things. Men can benefit from this book as well. Even if you have never considered turning the controls over to your wife, you may want to after you having read this book.

Take a moment to honestly answer the questions below:

1. Does your husband give you as much attention as he did when you were first married?

2. Does your husband do his share of the housework?

3. Is your sex-life as active (or satisfying) as it was when you first got married?

4. Do you always get your needs met, sexually speaking?

5. Is your husband as romantic as he once was?

If you answered, "Yes" to all these questions, take this book back to the store. Or put it away somewhere where you won't see it for at least a couple of years. You are most likely a newlywed and have no idea what's in store for you in the future.

On the other hand, if you answered, "No" to any of the above questions, you should read this book carefully and take notes. You may find that this book can be an invaluable tool in making your marriage the best that it can be.

Why do you want an FLR?

Let's be honest here. If you answered "No" to more than two of the questions above, there are things about your marriage that you would like to change. Most likely, you have no idea how to go about effecting those changes, either. With this book, you will learn how to take control of any or all aspects of your marriage and to improve both your sex life and the way your husband treats you. If he doesn't already treat you like a queen, then you need this book.

There is one thing I didn't mention before. It doesn't matter what you look like for your husband to want you, love you, and see you as his "Queen." In fact, using my methods, he will see you as the most beautiful woman in the world. I can say with certainty that he will because I, myself, have applied the principles of an FLR to my marriage and it has worked out well. I have also done a number of studies (not really scientific, though) that show that men would rather a have an over-weight, not so "model-looking" wife who knows how to keep him sexually aroused than the most beautiful woman he can think of.

Let's face it ladies (and gentlemen), men are sexually oriented beings. They are driven by their libidos (their sexual desires). This should be evident by the number of them who look at pornography, or are tempted to (or actually do) have affairs with other women. I'm not saying there is anything wrong with them, I just pointing out what should be obvious to most people. Because men are driven by their libidos, they are so easy to control. If you know the secret.

The fact is, men enjoy being lead around by their libidos. If you can do that, he will gladly follow you anywhere you want him to go, behave in any way you want him to behave, and do just about anything you want him to do. It's that simple, and this book will show you exactly how to do just that.

Why does *he* want an FLR?

If you are one of those women whose husband has mentioned that he would like you to take charge of some or all of your relationship, consider yourself lucky. Chances are, you blew him off, or thought he was getting too 'kinky' for you. Or he was so intimidated by you that he wasn't able to make himself clear. But if you did not take him up on his suggestion, shame on you. You passed up a chance to make your entire marriage better than you ever imagined it could be.

Many men would jump at the chance to let their wives take complete control of their lives. Most of them are too timid, or are afraid of what you will think of them if they come right out and ask. So, many of them suffer quietly. Others don't think they could ever submit to their wives by allowing her to be in charge of anything. But they have never experienced it.

I'll be honest with you. More honest than your husband could be, even if he came right out and asked you to become his Mistress, he doesn't care who is in charge. If you take the reins in the right way, he will not have to make all the big decisions. He won't have to worry about what you might think about things because he will know. Why? Because you will tell him.

He may tell you that he wants to improve your marriage. Or maybe that he wants to be a better husband. Or even that he wants to put the romance back into your marriage. He might even tell you that he wants to do more around the house for you. Whatever he says, is only a means to an end. After all, if he was actually driven by these desires, he could do it all without your help. The problem is, that is not his ultimate goal. He is not (at this point) driven by a desire to please you.

The truth is, he wants more sex. All men want more sex. Don't hold that against them, they can't help it. They were just made that way. But don't, for even a minute, think that just giving him more sex will satisfy him, or that it will change anything. It won't! He will still want more sex. Why? Because he doesn't understand what it is that he really wants.

To be fair about it, he may actually want all these things. After all, assuming he loves you, he might very well want to be a better husband. But those desires are not the driving force in his life. They are not what makes him get up in the morning and make, and serve you, breakfast in bed. They are not the sole reason why he does just about everything he does for you. Men just don't work that way.

The problem is, men think that in order for them to be sexually satisfied means that they must, necessarily, ejaculate (have an orgasm) in order to be happy. What they don't understand is their whole life their own bodies have told them this. So by now, they believe it. But it's just not true.

Most men think that the best part of sex is the ejaculation (or orgasm). They do not understand that it is really the build up to the orgasm that is (or should be) the most erotic and exciting part of any sexual activity.

But don't worry, you have the power to change everything and get the relationship you have always dreamed of having. Maybe you had it at first, but didn't realize it was gone. The fact remains, you want what he wants. The difference is, you have the power to get it. And you have the power to make him want it enough to act upon it.

You should want to be the one in charge of many aspects of your relationship. Maybe not all, but many of them at the very least. After all, if you could, wouldn't you want to change a few things? Wouldn't you want a more attentive husband? One who does at least *some* of the housework? One who takes more of an interest in the kids and what is going on in their lives? How about sex? Wouldn't it be nice if your husband spent more time making sure that your sexual needs were met *before* he even considered his own?

Well, if you could improve your relationship, your sex-life, your husbands attention to you, and even have a better marriage overall, wouldn't you do it? Then you want an FLR. You need to take charge of your relationship, your husband, and your sex-life. You owe it to yourself to read the rest of this book and at least try the basic principles that I will teach you. Then you can decide just how much (or how little) control you want.

What if he doesn't want an FLR?

So what if your husband has never indicated that he wants you to take charge of anything? Well, then you don't have to worry about discussing what he wants, do you? As I said before, all men want more sex. So if he is going to be getting more sex, why worry about telling him what is going on? After all, he will be happy. You will be happy. He won't realize what happened until it's too late to do anything about it.

There is another, very important thing that you need in order to begin the process, and that is the right attitude. Don't go into this with the attitude you are just going to change things so that you will be happier. You must keep in mind that your happiness requires not only your husband's happiness, but that your entire marriage and family life improve as well. That means you should always keep the ultimate goal in mind. You are not doing this just for you. You are doing it for your family and your marriage.

Why do I tell you this? Simply because I have seen many women lose sight of their true goal and end up just ruling over their husbands without taking his feelings into account. With some men, this is easy to do. With others it would be more difficult. But by keeping your ultimate goal in mind, that of improving your entire life and that of your family, then you stand a much better chance of success. And success is what we are after.

For you husbands reading this, those of you who have fantasized for years about leading this type of lifestyle, there are ways to convince your wife to take the reins and be the woman you want her to be. I have included a section on how to approach your wife in such a way that she will be willing to at least try to take control of things. So don't be discouraged because this book was written as guide to women. You can give it to your wife now, or wait until after you have approached her about this type of lifestyle.

You have the Power

If you genuinely want to change things for the better, you have the power. You may not realize it, but it has always been there. You just forgot how to use it. That, or you never realized it was there and used it without knowing what you were doing. I am talking about *Erotic Power*.

Erotic power is nothing new. Chances are, you used it when the two of you were dating and didn't even know it. Or at least, didn't know what it was called. That was a time when your husband was pursuing you. He would do anything to win your affection. Well, erotic power is what you are going to use again.

Somewhere along the line, shortly after you married perhaps, he stopped doing everything you asked. Why? Because you stopped using your erotic power over him. The two of you settled into a routine as far as sex was concerned. He was getting sex on a fairly regular basis. He had no need to pursue you. After all, you were married. Why would he need to pursue you? So you lost your power. You never even noticed. Now it's time you used that power again. After all, life was much better back then. Wasn't it?

Erotic power is the very heart of your control over your husband. It is the spark that ignites both his passion for you and yours for him. It is the means by which you will both be drawn together. It will strengthen your love for each other. Erotic power will become the mortar that binds your love and strengthens your marriage.

Everyone has a libido. We often call it "sex drive." It's an area of the brain that controls our desire for sex. Men are often driven by their libidos. It's one of the strongest factors that effects his behavior. It can subvert his ego and make him do things he would not otherwise do. Erotic power gives you a direct line to his libido. By controlling his libido, you control him. It has been said that a man thinks about sex once every six minutes. It's probably more like every six seconds, but whatever the frequency, the libido is a powerful, and persistent part of a man's brain.

The problem most men have is understanding their own sexual drive. I am not talking about what turns him on, I am talking about what he *thinks* he wants. He thinks he wants to ejaculate (have an orgasm), but as soon as he does, his desire for sex will come to an abrupt end. You see, when a man gets sexually excited, certain hormones and endorphins are released by the brain. Without going into all the boring detail, suffice it to say, as soon as he ejaculates (in a normal fashion) different hormones are released and he loses his erection, his desire for sex, and he pretty much runs out of energy. His brain and his body tell him to rest.

What he needs to learn is that the build up to ejaculation is far more enjoyable than the actual orgasm itself. This being the case, it is up to you to teach him and his body the truth. He needs to learn that life is much more enjoyable when he is aroused. It's your job to keep him aroused. The more he is aroused, more he will enjoy life. The more he enjoys life, the more he will be willing to do for you. And that is your goal.

However, every man is different. Men are driven by different sexual stimuli. Basically, he will fantasize about the different things that stimulate him the most. But we will discuss his fantasies, in depth, a little later. What you need to know is that a man will follow his libido almost anywhere it leads him. Since you have a direct line to his libido, you can take it (and him) anywhere you want it to go. It is your responsibility to take control of his libido!

If left unchecked, a man's libido can lead him to cheat on his wife even though he loves her very much. It can cause him to spend hours looking at pornography on the Internet or purchase "dirty" magazines to satisfy himself. Masturbation is the enemy of Erotic Power. If a man masturbates too often, his desire for you (and sex) will diminish. Therefore, you will need to reduce his desire to masturbate by replacing it with something even more desirable. Barring that, I have two words for you... Male Chastity. We will cover male chastity in depth in a later chapter.

The secret to using your erotic power is to gradually introduce some suggestions. He will follow those suggestions as long as his libido tells him to. That is, he will be willing to do more for you in order to reach his ultimate goal... sexual gratification. In simple terms, he won't be able to resist you, or the chores you want him to perform. As long as he anticipates a sexual reward, he will gladly do anything you desire. And that's the key to your new found power and your control over him and the happiness you will enjoy in your future.

Men often regard washing dishes as "woman's work." So, even though he may wash them, he may only be doing it as a "favor" to you. Unless... You use your erotic power. Use that direct line to his libido. Remember, with the expectation of sexual gratification, a man will do the most humiliating things willingly! He will even enjoy it.

Exactly what you do, or how far you push him using your new found power, is entirely up to you. He may not even resist you. Your main enemy in the use of this power is you. Many women have guilt feelings because of societal taboos and upbringing. You have to find the confidence to use your power. You must learn to wield your power. Only then can you wield it in any way you like. Of course, you will also take your husband's feelings into account. That is, you could probably get him to embarrass himself in public. But would you really want to do that? Probably not. Though it is unlikely that you would abuse your power, after all, you love your husband, but at the same time, you don't want to fail at controlling him because you are too timid. I will go into more detail on this in a later chapter.

This is NOT a one-sided relationship. Your marriage should be a partnership. Think of it as I mentioned before, you are the Queen and he is your Knight in shinning armor. It is a partnership where you are in charge and he willingly does your bidding. Don't think for a moment that you will not have to do anything. On the contrary, you will have to do more (sexually) than you are currently doing. But don't let that put you off.

You will enjoy what you are going to do and your needs will be met *before* his.

The complement of your power, your erotic power, is your husband's willingness to submit to your will and authority. Through your gradual, yet firm control, your husband will obey your wishes. He will bend to your will. He will happily help you create the wonderful, even joyous, relationship you both want and deserve.

So you must do your part. You must take control of him and your sexual desires in order to create a more perfect relationship between the two of you. Think of it as a barter system, the more you give, the more you get. If you can't do this for yourself, do it for your children, your husband, your marriage. But make no mistake, like in any barter system, the more you want from your husband, the more you will have to give him. In this case, however, we are bartering sexual gratification, for obedience.

If you think about it, I am sure you can think of many more things that you can do with your new-found power. What do you want? The car washed once a week? Someone to do all the vacuuming? The dishes washed every night? How about someone to clean the bathrooms for you? Think about it. Make a list of things that you would like your husband to do for you. He isn't going to do them all the first time out, but eventually, he will do whatever you want. So don't hesitate to include everything. Even those foot and back rubs you enjoy so much. And, perhaps, a minimum number of orgasms for yourself.

When you are ready, you can begin with a few of the easier tasks and work your way through the list. By the time you have taken total control of your husband, you will have made up a whole new list.

What you want to be is his object of worship. Not in a literal sense, but in an idyllic marriage sense. What you will be doing is simply giving him what he wants in return for him doing what you want. You are going to give him all the sex he wants, but you are going to dole it out in small portions. Like dangling a carrot in front of an ass (pun intended).

Many women find it difficult, for one reason or another, to take charge of their relationship. Remember your wedding vows? Did they include something about "for better or worse?" Well, draw in a deep breath and summon all your courage, because this is for the *better*. If, while doing the things I instruct you to do, you can keep in mind that all this is going to make your marriage better, you can find the courage to make it happen.

You will learn how to do this as we go along, so don't worry. Another benefit of learning to use your erotic power is the confidence you will gain from it. You may become more confident and assertive at work (assuming you have a job). You may also notice how it helps you in other areas of your life. If you are not already a confident, assertive individual, learning to use your erotic power can help.

Talk, Talk, Talk!

Communication is the single most important aspect of any successful relationship. You can ask any marriage expert in the Western hemisphere and they will agree. For your relationship to be completely successful, you will have to become good at communicating with your husband, and getting him to communicate with you. You'll find getting him to talk may be easier than opening up yourself.

The power is within you. All you have to do is summon the strength to use it. As you will see in later chapters, you will be able to do that, one step at a time. You will be learning to control your husband just as he will be learning to accept your control. So take a deep breath, and tell yourself with all the conviction you can muster, "I can do this because I have the power!" Repeat it everyday. Say it in front of the mirror. Remind yourself as often as you can, that you can do it, because you have the power.

If your lack of confidence stems from any other reason, remember, we are going to start slow, and your confidence will grow as you progress. You will be in charge of how fast, or how slow, you progress. Of course, everyone is different, and things may need to be adjusted accordingly. So if your husband doesn't respond as quickly as you would like, be patient, he will reach the point where you want him, eventually.

One thing you are going to learn to do is to talk during sex. If you are not comfortable doing that, perhaps because you have never done it, or because you are not comfortable talking about sex with your husband, you will have to draw upon your determination, your desire to change things, in order to be successful. But never fear, I will show you how to overcome your shyness.

If your fear stems from a feeling of guilt, keep reminding yourself that your husband is going to love the results of your actions. If you feel guilty because you will be denying him a few things he has a "right" to, remember that you will be giving him more sex than he ever thought he would get. You're just going to dole it out in smaller doses. How much he gets depends entirely on his behavior and cooperation with what you want. Think of it as training a dog. It works the same way.

So what you have to do, is ask yourself, "Do I want to make my marriage better? Do I want a more attentive husband? Do I want a better sex life?" if you can answer, "Yes" to any of these questions, then you owe it to yourself and your family to summon your courage and determination to overcome your feelings of guilt or lack of confidence. You CAN do this!

If your husband has indicated that he would like you to take charge of ANYTHING in your marriage, he may be wanting this. If he has said any of the following words or phrases in a sexual context, you can begin by discussing your plans with him. Words like: chastity, cock teasing, orgasm denial, orgasm control, tease and denial, or even female lead relationship, then he may already be willing to give you the control you seek. If not, then you may have to "spring" it on him after you have him hooked.

Let's assume he has mentioned one or more of these things, before. Chances are that you could simply sit down and discuss exactly what he has in mind. You don't have to tell him what you have in mind, but knowing what he wants puts you a step ahead. If he has had fantasies about being controlled by you (or any woman) he will be open to you taking control. Of course, he may want to start out slowly, which is just fine with you. Or he may want to jump in with both feet. Either way, don't agree to anything other than giving it a try. You can figure out just how much control you want to take later. Besides, he is going to do what you want, not what he wants.

If he has never mentioned anything like this before, take heart, he will love it once you get started. But you might not want to discuss your plans with him at this point, because he may just tell you that he wants nothing to do with it all. The truth is, he has never experienced anything like what you are going to be doing with (to) him, so he really doesn't know. And at this point, the less he knows, the better.

Another area where many women have difficulty is talking in bed. Especially talking "dirty." Some women don't talk at all, about anything. That just won't do. You are going to have to learn to relax enough to say anything to your husband during sex, no matter how "dirty" it may seem. I know that for some of you, that will be difficult. But I will show you a way to learn to do it that will be easy, even if you have never talked in bed before. In fact, you are going to start by getting him to talk to you. That way, it will be much easier for you to talk as well.

By taking small steps, you will learn to take total control over, not only your sex life, but all aspects of your marriage as well. Like I said before, you take as much or as little control as you would like, but I will show you everything you need to know. That way, you will have a better idea of just how much control you wish to wield.

During your first tease session, the goal will not be how long you can go, nor will it be to deny your husband an orgasm. Your goal, during that first session, will be to get your husband to open up to you. I will show you how to do that. We're not quite ready for that, just yet. The easiest way to get him talking is to ask him questions.

When you get to the point in this book (or your relationship) that you are ready for your first session, you will want to ask him lots of questions. Ask him if he remembers how things were when you were dating or when you were newlyweds. Ask him if he is totally happy with your current sex-life. Ask him if he would like to improve your relationship. Basically, ask him the same questions I asked you at the beginning of this book. Ask him if he would like to turn your relationship into something more like it was when you first got married. Ask if he would like to have more attention from you. Ask if he would like to have more sex than he has been getting lately. I don't know a man in the world who wouldn't want more sex, so be sure he answers you honestly.

If he indicates that he would like to improve your marriage. Ask if he would be willing try a little experiment. Tell him that you have something in mind and that you would like him to bear with you while you try something new. Remember, you should ask these questions when you are in bed. If you can, ask them while you are 'playing' with his genitals. You will not only have is undivided attention, but if he likes what you are doing, and chances are he will, then he should be willing to try anything.

By asking him questions, you will learn to talk more during sex. (See how easy that was?) Let him ask you some questions, because he will have questions. How much you tell him about your plans is up to you, but at this point, it's best not to reveal much about your plans. Simply tell him that you want to try a little experiment and you don't want to spoil the surprise by telling about it. Simply tell him that are planning to do a little sexual experiment and that you are sure he will enjoy it. Let it go at that. The less he knows, at this point, the better.

So, when you finally get to your first tease session, you should be more relaxed about having to do all the talking. You won't have to. The more you can get him to talk, the less you will need to talk. But you will become more and more at ease talking about sex. Before long, you will be perfectly at ease saying anything to your husband. And that is good, because later, you need to do more talking than you have probably ever done before.

When your husband agrees that he wants to try to improve things, all you need to tell him is that you want to try an experiment that includes more sex. Once he agrees to try it, you are done. Don't tell him what the experiment is, just that you will both get more sex and that, if it works, everything will get better. Let that be all the information he gets, for now.

Psychology 101

As you will recall from a previous chapter, men are driven by their libidos. Because of this, their entire outlook on life is different from a woman's. One thing his libido does is cause him to fantasize. Those fantasies will vary from man to man and even from day to day in the same man. My point here, is that a man's fantasies are ever changing (evolving) from day to day, week to week, and month the month. Knowing these fantasies can greatly enhance your erotic power over him and thus, they are an important tool for you to use in controlling him.

Every man has fantasies. They are as individual as snowflakes. That is, no two men have exactly the same fantasies. The important thing to remember here is that your husband has fantasies that you know nothing about. Remember, it's not his fault what his fantasies entail, it is only important that you learn what they are and how to make him fantasize about you!

Chances are, your husband's fantasies don't include you. Don't take offense at that. Remember, up until now, his libido has driven his fantasies in many random directions. Also, don't condemn him if his fantasies are about things that might be illegal or even immoral. Keep in mind, as long as he does not act on his fantasies, they are harmless. They are like random thoughts. We all have them. Sometimes they are nice, sometimes they are not. But what pops into our heads can't always be controlled.

For example, a common fantasy that many men share is one in which the object of his arousal is an under-age girl. A school girl perhaps. As long as he does not hang around playgrounds and schools where he has no business being, it's okay. As long as he does not proposition young girls, he is not (necessarily) a pervert. Sometimes it is hard to accept some of the fantasies men have. That's why they often don't want to reveal them to us. But you must find a way passed that. As I said, he can't help what turns him only what he does about it.

What is important is that you discover what his favorite fantasies are and use them to help you gain control of him. No, not through black-mail or anything like that. I know there are women out there who do things like that. Please, don't become one of them. You need to gain his trust. Black-mailing him because of his fantasies is NOT the way to do that.

Odds are, even if he does have immoral fantasies, he isn't going to tell you about them. That's okay, he doesn't need to. At least not at this point. Unless he has an unhealthy obsession over one of his fantasies, don't be concerned about them. Your objective is to get him to open up about his fantasies and to allow you to become a part of them.

Fantasies are important. Why? Because your husband is going to have them no matter what you try to do to discourage him. So instead of discouraging him, you need to encourage him. The difference is, you are going to put yourself into his fantasies. You are going to become the object of his sexual desires. That's what gives you the most erotic power over him.

Another important fact about a man's fantasies is that in every one of them, there is another person. I have not heard very many men say that they fantasize about masturbation, unless it's in a humiliating setting such as forced masturbation or even public masturbation. What that means is, most likely, there is a woman in his fantasies. It may not always be the same woman, and exactly who she might be will change from time to time. She may not even have a face. He may not know her name. But the point is, you will become that woman!

In other words, the woman whom he dreams about most often, will change over time. For example, there might be a time when his fantasy woman resembles a famous model because he saw a photo of her dressed a certain way. A month or so later he might see an actress portraying a particularly sexy role and the woman in his fantasies will become her. Often times, a man will not be able to tell you exactly who the woman in his fantasies is because she actually is a conglomerate of several women. She may even have no face at all.

My point is this, no matter who or what he fantasizes about, you can become the woman in those fantasies. And that is exactly what you are going to do. After all, wouldn't you like him to fantasize about you? Well, that is the fastest way to get control of his libido... Through his fantasies. You want him to think about you every time he has a fantasy (which is several times a day, by the way). Once you put yourself into his fantasies you will be able to guide and control those fantasies so that he will think of you as the only woman who can please him.

Obviously, you are going to need to know his favorite fantasies. You will need him to tell you what those fantasies are. It isn't important who is currently the object of his fantasies, because you are going to put yourself into them. You will replace that other person (real or imagined) with yourself. Pay attention, this is the most important part of controlling your husband's sexual desires and, therefore, his libido.

Okay, so just how do you find out what his fantasies are? The most obvious answer is to ask him. But if you ask him over dinner, you will, most likely, not get any useful information, unless, of course, he feels that he can tell you anything. No, the time and place for getting his fantasies out of him is in the bedroom when he is the most sexually excited.

Let's face it, many men have divulged secrets, even vital information about national security, to a woman during sex. It's an historical fact. So getting him to tell you his secrets should be easy in comparison, don't you think? The best method of prying information about his fantasies from him will be during sex.

What you will do, is simple. While you are pleasing (teasing) him, you will have his undivided attention. That's when you start asking him questions. You will ask about his fantasies, and you will NOT judge him or demean him because of those fantasies. Remember, you should not really be concerned with the content of his fantasies, except to help you gain control of his libido. He may even surprise you by having fantasies about being sexually controlled by a woman. Many men do. In fact, that would be a good question to ask him. "Has he ever had fantasies in which he is controlled by a woman?"

If a man experiences a great deal of pressure at work, if he has to make many important decisions, he may very well have fantasies about being controlled by a woman. Many professional Mistresses will tell you that a great number of businessmen use their services in order to relieve the stress of their jobs.

You may actually discover that your husband is one of those men who has used a professional dominatrix before. If you do, though you have a perfect right to get angry, maybe even divorce him, I urge you NOT to condemn him for it. After all, men are weak when it comes to their libidos. And you can use that information to move along more quickly. He already enjoys having a woman in charge, so why not be that woman? Besides, aren't you reading this book in order to make your marriage better?

While you have your man in bed, in a position where you can fondle his penis and balls, it's a good time to start the ball rolling (figuratively). Ask him about his fantasies. Don't let him get away with telling you he doesn't have them. He does. He just doesn't want to tell you about them. You may have to reassure him that you are not going to judge him. Tell him that you want to know what he fantasizes about so that you can enjoy them, too. Press him for details. You need to know as much as you can find out. For example, if your husband says he has a fantasy about a woman who gives him a really great blow-job. By pressing for details, you may discover that what really turns him on is not so much the act itself, but what the woman is wearing that gets him all excited. So press for details!

Once you know your husband's fantasies, it will be easy to put yourself into them. All you have to do is tell him a favorite fantasy of his, but put yourself into the fantasy. For example, if the outfit the woman in his fantasy was wearing turns him on, tell him that you are wearing that outfit (or, better yet, actually wear it). If you do this while you are teasing him in bed, he will soon begin to replace the other woman in his fantasy with you, every time he has that fantasy. And that, ladies, is your first goal!

If your husband is one of those who is too shy to tell you his fantasies, even while you are teasing his penis in bed, there are other ways of getting this information. For instance, if he visits porn sites on the web, check his history and find out what kinds of sites he visits. Do they have a theme such as school girls, spanking, domination, etc.? Armed with this information you can begin making up your own fantasies using what you have learned.

Another method is to have him send you to some web sites that he likes. Perhaps he can give you links to certain stories, or types of photos that turn him on. Maybe he will be willing to write out a fantasy and send it to you in an email or even a letter. Be aware, he may test you at first by telling you some of his "not-so-kinky" fantasies to see how you react. If all goes well, he may be more willing to open up to you and tell you those deep, dark ones that he has been afraid to reveal. Again, don't judge him because of the fantasies he has.

Another method of getting him to open up to you, and tell you what really turns him on is to ask questions. Ask him about his first erotic experience with sex. Was it a dream? Was it something that happened to him as a teenager. Ask him if he ever has any erotic dreams now and get him to tell you about them. Talking to him is the best way to to put, not only him, at ease, but yourself as well. Asking questions will help you become more at ease with talking in bed. Especially if you have a problem with that.

Whatever method you use, be sure you do not make him feel self-conscious about telling you. If you make him think that you are appalled by his fantasies, he will clam up and refuse to tell you any more of them. It is so important that he feel that he can tell you anything without fear of being ridiculed or put down because of his fantasies. Prepare yourself for the worst. Then maybe you won't be so shocked when he tells you his favorite fantasy. Remember, it's not what he fantasizes, it's whether or not he has ever acted upon them. You will have to give him a great deal of reassurance that whatever his fantasies are, you will not be shocked or upset with him.

Let's look at one example, shall we. Suppose you discover that your husband frequents web sites that feature stories or photos of men having sex with "school girls". Pretty shocking, right? Instead of yelling and screaming at him for doing that (which will stop once you have control), try making up a fantasy to tell him about you forcing him to have sex with a young school girl.

Remember, it's probably the outfit she is wearing, rather than her age, that turns him on the most. Eventually, you will be able to remove the "girls" from the fantasy and replace them with yourself. Another method would be to wear an outfit similar to the ones in his fantasy the next time you want to tease him. That almost always works.

The point I am trying to make is this: no matter what your husband fantasizes about, you can put yourself into those fantasies, which is the first step toward controlling him and his behavior. And that is the ultimate goal. By putting yourself into his fantasies (along with a few other things we will discuss), you will be on his mind a great deal more than you have been in the past. The more you are in his sexual dreams (or fantasies) the more control you will have over him.

In another chapter I will teach you how to put him in the mood to talk. To tell you his fantasies so that you can begin to understand what turns him on.

Getting Started

Seduction has a very romantic connotation. After all, it brings to mind the romance of one partner pursuing the other. It implies so much. First and foremost, it implies that the pursued is attractive and desirable to the pursuer. Well, that's exactly what you want. So that's what you are going to do. You are going to pursue your husband.

You know (or at least you think you know) what he likes... Sexually speaking. Use that to get him into bed with you. You are going to pursue your husband for the first couple of weeks. This will serve two purposes; 1) It will make him realize that you still love him and want sex with him; and 2) It will allow you to extract information that you will need later. Remember? We talked about that.

You are also going to be learning to talk during sex. Don't be frightened by that. It will be easier than you think. Information is power! All you are going to be doing is gathering information to increase the erotic power you already have.

Warming Him Up

Romance is closely linked to seduction. The best way to warm him up is to seduce him. Start early in the day by dropping little hints that you are in a romantic mood. Pick a day and time when you know you can be alone (loan the kids out, or hire a babysitter) so that you can go out by yourselves. Plan a dinner out, even if all you can afford is a fast-food restaurant. You might be surprised at how little the location has to do with it. (My husband proposed to me in a McDonald's restaurant.) You might even want to stay home and prepare a romantic evening at home.

While on your "date," remind him of some of the romantic things he did, or that you did together, when you were first dating. Reminiscing is a good way to get him thinking about the future. Tell him how wonderful you felt at that time. Ask him what he remembers of that time. Keep your dinner conversation focused on your early years or any time when sex was more frequent. Ask him if he would like to have more sex. Tell him you love him and that you would like to re-ignite the fire you both once had for each other. Ask if he would like that, too.

Then, when you are ready, retire to the bedroom. You don't want to try to do anything special. That is, don't try to get him to do anything special for you. If he is willing to please you, great! If not, don't worry too much about it now. Your chance will come. In fact, you are only trying to establish the fact that you still love him and that you want things to change. Change for the better.

In his mind, confusion may set in. That's good. You want to catch and keep him off balance. After this first seduction, you want to initiate sex at least two or three times a week for the next two to three weeks. He won't understand what is going on, and if he asks you about it, just say that you want to show him how much you love him. Allow him to initiate sex if he wants. After all, he has a limited time to do that before you take control.

You may be wondering why you are giving him everything he wants. The answer is simple, while you are preparing to take total control over him, his sex-life, and your marriage, he will be happily thinking that he likes the changes you have made. Of course, in a matter of a few of weeks, he is going to begin to lose all the control he now "thinks" he has. So just tell him you are performing an experiment and ask him if he is enjoying it, so far.

You don't have to do this for long. As I said, in a few of weeks, you are going to make some changes. You are going to do it, slowly, gently, and without his even knowing that things have changed until it's too late for him to do anything about it. Don't miss a chance to talk during these sessions.

If you can, ask him questions related to what you are doing. Ask if he likes it when you fondle his genitals, or do some other activity. While attempting to get him to talk, you should be becoming more comfortable with talking, as well. You should, at some point, ask if he ever has any sexual fantasies. You don't need to probe for specifics, at this point, because he may not be ready to tell you about them, anyway. Any information you glean from him will be useful later. So take some mental notes as you go.

After the first week you will want to change things a little. You need to get some important information from him. You need to get him telling you, at least some of his fantasies. I suggest you try the following technique. Have him lay on his back with his legs spread wide apart. Tell him to grab hold of the pillow behind his head and ask him to keep his hands there while you try a little experiment. Find yourself a comfortable position. Sitting between his legs with your legs over his works very well. It traps his legs and prevents him from moving too much. Later, you may want to try a little bondage to keep him in place. That allows you a little more freedom of movement, too.

Now, put some lubrication on your hands (KY Jelly® or baby oil work well for this). You want to begin by very slowly and VERY gently fondling his penis. I don't recommend doing much stroking as this may suddenly end your session before you are ready if he should lose control and have an orgasm. While you are fondling his penis and balls, ask him questions. Ask him what his favorite fantasy is. Press him to tell you as much detail as you can squeeze out of him. Your goal is not orgasm! It's information. So be careful not to stimulate him too much. If you suspect that he is getting too aroused, simply stop touching his genitals. Instead, try fondling, even lightly pinching, his nipples. Make him tell you some sexual secret before touching his genitals again. Give him at least a full minute to rest before you touch his genitals again.

You want this teasing to last for at least thirty minutes. An hour or more would be even better. When you are ready to end your session, begin a steady, yet slow, stroking of his penis. Be sure to keep him well lubricated during the entire session. Just add lubrication when needed to keep his genitals very slippery. As your guy begins to approach his orgasm, speed up your stroking. Hopefully, he will explode when he does finally reach orgasm (ejaculation). That's what you want. Once he has had his orgasm, allow him a few minutes of rest before you clean him up. Use a dry wash rag to clean up. I find it works best. While he is resting, it's a good time to ask if he enjoyed what you did to him. Tell him that there will be lots more of that kind of thing to come, in the near future.

If you continue to do this every session for the next few weeks, you should be able to gather quite a bit of information about his fantasies. If you paid close attention, and did NOT make any negative comments about his fantasies, then you should have some idea what gets him excited. You need to pay attention to any specific details he gives you. You never know what is important and what is not. For example, if he specifically mentions what the woman in his fantasy is wearing, or something she uses (such as a riding crop), you can bet your bottom dollar (or whatever currency you use) that it's very important to getting him aroused. Don't forget, you can always ask him questions while he is telling you his fantasy. Stop him to ask what the woman is wearing, or ask him to describe the item she is using in more detail. You may even want to take notes, later when you have the time.

For now, just be content with letting him think things are going his way. Little does he know that you will soon have him wrapped around your little finger and he will be loving it... And he will be loving you for it.

During the course of these few weeks, pay attention to your husband. Show him you love him by doing little things you know he likes. Whisper in his ear that you love him anytime you get the opportunity. Make little suggestive remarks, too. Things like, "Are you going to be up for sex tonight?" Or, "I've been thinking about what we did the other night and I can't wait for the next time." You can even get more graphic if you like. Use some "dirty" talk, you know will turn him on.

The point of all this attention is to keep his mind on you (and sex). Later, there will be other things of this sort that you will need to do on a daily basis, that are designed to keep his mind where you want it. But for now, it's just good practice. By the time you are ready to start taking control, you will be much more comfortable talking 'dirty' and talking in bed.

Once your husband has been properly warmed up by all this attention, you will be ready to proceed with more serious teasing and even some denial.

Methods of Teasing

Teasing a man sexually is an easy and fun thing to do. In fact, you should do all you can to find a way to really enjoy it. If you think of it as a game, perhaps that will make it easier. Remember, in the beginning, you will have to work on it. It may come easy to you, and it may not. But once you have him under control, it will be his job to make sure that you are rewarded for having taken control. He will love doing it, even if he gets less in return. In all likelihood, he will get very turned on every time he pleases you sexually. And that will work to your advantage.

The trick to proper teasing, is knowing how to do it. Here are some simple methods to get you started. Bear in mind, the most important thing you can do is to vary how you tease him. Use your imagination. Talk to him. Tell him one of his favorite fantasies. Maybe even tell him a new one using what you have learned from him so far. If you are still too timid to tell him one of his favorite fantasies, have him tell it to you. Maybe he has a new one he hasn't told you, yet. This will keep his mind on what you are doing.

Remember, when teasing him, the objective is not to allow an orgasm until you are done. Once he ejaculates, he is finished. You should, at this point, allow him to ejaculate, but NOT until you have teased him for as long as you can stand to do it. I recommend at least thirty minutes to an hour. Longer, if you can. Another tip; Try blindfolding him. Taking away his sight can enhance his sense of toucch!

- The Soft Touch: This method of teasing requires no lubrication. You are not even going to use your hands to touch his body. Instead, use a very soft brush (a soft paint brush or a cosmetic brush). Brush it very lightly over his genitals, his nipples, even his torso. If he is too ticklish in spots, try to avoid those areas. The object is to turn him on not distract him from your goal. Hopefully, you will not be able to make him ejaculate strictly using the brush. If you have angora gloves (or anything made of angora) try that. It has such a soft feel that it should drive him crazy.

- Soft Strokes: Try lubricating his penis and touching it so lightly that he will not be able to achieve ejaculation. Don't grip his penis at all. Instead, let it rest on your fingers and slide them up and down the length of it VERY slowly. Again, the objective is to do it so lightly that he will not be able to reach orgasm. At least, not until you want him to.

- Toothpick Tease: Find yourself a nice wooden toothpick or wooden kabob skewer. You want a point on the end but not one so sharp it might pierce the skin. Now, gently poke his skin. Poke his scrotum, his penis, his nipples, and any other place you can find. Don't forget to poke the inside of his thighs gently. The area behind his scrotum can be very sensitive, as well. If you have him stretched out as I described in the chapter on "*Getting Started*," you can also poke his sides a bit. Always do this gently at first. If he seems to respond positively to more firm poking, then you can do that as well.

- Feather Tease: If you can get yourself an ostrich feather, you have got to try it. Ostrich feathers can often be purchased from craft shops or through your favorite adult sex shop. If you can't get an ostrich feather, any other feather, such as a feather duster, will work, too. Again, you want to gently rake it across his body, paying special attention to his genitals. If his nipples are sensitive, give them some attention, too. Any place that draws a reaction is a good place to drag your feather. It should be very difficult, especially if you are paying close attention, for him to ejaculate with the feather alone.

- Teasing with Ice: Ice, when placed in a zip-lock bag can also be used to tease your guy. It tends to help him stave off an ejaculation as well as chill his body. Don't hold the ice in any one spot for more than few seconds as it will quickly become uncomfortable. The only possible exception is his penis. Used properly, you can cause him to lose all or part of his erection be applying ice directly to his penis. Our goal, though, is to keep him erect and on the verge of ejaculating, if possible. (The zip-lock bag keeps everything from getting all wet.)

- Stroke & Stop Method: Yes, it's exactly what it sounds like. All you have to do is give his penis a few strokes, then stop. You can use this method to tease him by only a few strokes with a 30 second to one minute break between. Later, you may want to use this method to determine just when he is about to ejaculate and then keep him from doing it. It's called 'edging,' and it can be quite useful when you want your husband to beg you to allow him to ejaculate. (A very fun thing to do, by the way.)

- Popsicle Tease: Like the ice tease above, the Popsicle tease can be used to help stave off an orgasm. You need to have a dry cloth handy, however, since the Popsicle will not be in a zip-lock bag. In this tease, you rub the Popsicle over any part of his body and follow it with your tongue. If you place it in areas that you can't reach with your tongue, use the cloth to wipe it off. The object is to replace the cold of the Popsicle with the warmth of your mouth. This will cause opposite sensations that can be very erotic to the subject. Again, don't let him ejaculate until you are ready.

- Verbal Teasing: Yes, you read that right. You can tease your husband any time, anywhere, as long as you can talk with him. Talk softly, right into his ear. Tell him romantic things, or down right sexual things. It's good practice and he will love it, especially if he cannot (for whatever reason) touch himself. You can tell him a fantasy, one of his or one of your own. You will need to practice this anyway, for future, daily teasing that you will need to do.

That should be enough to get you started. It is important to vary your method of teasing whenever you tease your partner. You don't want him to get bored or complacent by using the same method each time you tease him.

I suggest that, whenever you plan to tease your husband, have him satisfy you before you begin your teasing. However, if the only way you can be satisfied is through intercourse, I suggest you forgo your own satisfaction (for now). Remember, once he ejaculates, it's all over. So be sure that whatever you do, or have him do, will not risk him ejaculating.

There are other methods of teasing, but I'll leave it up to you and your imagination to figure out what else works for you and your husband. If you can't think of any other ways to tease him, the above listed teases should be enough to keep you both going for a long time.

The really important thing is that you tease your husband often. I recommend at least twice a week for thirty minutes or more. Don't forget all those daily teases, either. They are extremely important. If you want to maintain maximum erotic power over him, the more you tease, the better. I can't emphasize enough just how important teasing is. All I can do is suggest you find out for yourself. Fail to tease him for a few days, and you will see the result.

He will become less interested in serving your needs and begin to mope around. He may begin to think that you don't really care about all the things you said were important when the two of you embarked on this mission to improve your marriage.

Daily Teasing

I cannot stress enough how important it is to keep your man thinking about sex and (especially) YOU! After all, the whole point of teasing is to keep your guy horny and attentive. Attentive to both your sexual needs and desires and to the everyday chores you want him to perform around the house. Maybe I am going into too much detail, here, but I think it's really needed. While some things may seem obvious to some, others will be glad I was detailed.

The best way to accomplish this is to make and KEEP him as sexually aroused as possible as much of the time as possible. So let's talk about things you can do to keep him that way. The following are some examples of things you can do to insure that he will be thinking about you and about that next orgasm if and when you decide to give it to him. (Some things might not apply if your guy is in chastity.)

Before you send hubby off to work in the morning, put a note in his pocket, lunch bag, or brief case, somewhere he will be sure to find it after he has left the house. The note could be anything from a simple romantic "I love you" note, or it could include instructions for one or more of the other activities I will mention. You might say something like, "I can't wait until you get home because I want to play with your penis." Or it might say, "At lunch, I want you to go into the bathroom and masturbate for five minutes, but don't ejaculate! I want to play with you later, and I'll take care of that part."

Instead of a note, you might just send a text message to his cell phone, or call him if you like. Even if you use the note idea, it would be a good idea to call or text him several times during the day. Two or three text messages designed to arouse him will go a long way towards keeping his mind on you during the day. Try sending him to work with a small butt-plug (and some lubricant) and then call or text him when you want him to insert it. Make him put it in an hour or two before he comes home so you can check that he did as he was told.

You can also try sending him to work wearing a pair of silky panties under his clothes. If yours won't fit him, buy (or better yet) have him buy a pair that does fit. You could even have him buy them on his lunch break and put them on while still at work. Make him take *Tiger Balm®* or *Icy-Hot®* to work with him and then make him apply it to his penis, balls or anus at some point during the day. That should keep him thinking about you.

One last idea for the working man. Send him on an errand. Have him stop by your favorite lingerie store and buy something for you. If you really want to humiliate him, make him buy a blow-up doll with all the features (Greek, French, etc.). There are things you can make him do with it once he gets it home as well, but that's another book altogether.

So what do you do when you are both at home? Well, if you have no kids, it's easy. Make him spend some time naked while you remain fully dressed. Don't let him spend that time in the bedroom, either. Make him vacuum the living room, or wash the dishes, fix you dinner or even serve you sexually while you relax and watch a movie. There is no limit to what you can do with him when you have no children around. But just because you do have them, doesn't mean that there is nothing you can do.

If you have kids around the house try whispering something sexy like, "I would love to suck your penis right now." Especially if it really isn't feasible at the moment. Also, take every opportunity to fondle him through his clothing. It will turn him on and you can do it almost every time you pass each other.

Invite him into the bedroom and give him a quick blow-job. Don't let him ejaculate, just get him hard and ready for it, then tell him you will finish it later (or not). You can send him to the bathroom with orders to insert a plug or to get himself hard and wait for you. You can surely find a few minutes to sneak off from the kids long enough to tease him in some way, just for a few minutes. Use your imagination and see what you can come up with. All you are wanting to do is give him a few minutes of teasing. Nothing more. You should do these things as often as you can during the day.

If you use everything at your disposal, your man should never be a few seconds away from thinking about you and what you might have in store for him later. You know what turns him on, use it. Use his fantasies to get his imagination working overtime. It's really not that difficult if you put your mind to it. The hard part is remembering to keep at it! Don't let an opportunity to tease him slip by. The more you do this, the better you will get at doing it and it will soon become second nature.

Okay, Let's sum up; You have your husband in the palm of your hand (instead of his own). But how can you keep him interested in pleasing you all day, everyday? You need to come up with some ideas on how you can tease him, humiliate him, or just plain make him think about getting into bed with you, all day long. Here are a few ideas that sum up what we have been talking about. Of course, you can always think up a few ideas of your own.

While he is at work:

- Make him wear a pair of woman's panties to work under his regular clothes. Believe me, he will think about you all day!

- Send him text messages at random times telling him erotic things, such as, how much you want to suck his penis, or in what way you want him to give you an orgasm.

- While you're at it, have him stop by your favorite sex shop and pick up something that will embarrass him to buy. A vibrator, a butt-plug, a cock-ring, or a blowup doll perhaps?

- Call him on his cell phone and have him go to the rest room and masturbate while he is talking to you. Don't allow him to ejaculate, but make sure he has to do some talking. That will embarrass him if anyone should overhear.

- Have him put a plug in his butt for an hour or two. Or put one in before he goes to work and call him to tell him when he can take it out.

- Stick a pair of your panties in his pocket and tell him to fondle them, look at them or smell them several times during the day. Maybe when you call or text him?

When he is at home:

- Make him spend the day naked while doing chores.

- Make him masturbate for you but don't allow him to ejaculate.

- Make him beg to kiss your bottom.

- Put a leash on his penis and lead him around the house.

- Make him satisfy you orally several times during the day.

- Tie him to a chair and tease his penis for hours on end.

If you have kids at home:

- Call him into your bedroom several times during the day. Fondle or suck on his penis until it's really hard, then tell him he can go.

- Whisper in his ear that he is to go into your room and make himself hard. Have him call you when he has done it so that you can check the results.

- Take him to the bathroom and make him masturbate for you. Just don't let him ejaculate.

- Send him to the grocery store (or wherever) with a butt-plug in place.

- Make him wear a pair of woman's panties then stick your hand down his pants periodically and fondle him or his bottom through the panties.

- If you have two computers in the house, use your IM's to chat and build a fantasy together.

There are a million and one things that you can do to keep his mind on you and keep him sexually aroused. Use your imagination and I am sure you will be able to come up some ideas of your own. Don't be shy. After all, he is your husband.

Tease & Denial

Why Tease?

We have discussed many ways to tease your husband, and even the main reason for doing it. But I thought I would reiterate for you once again. The point of teasing is to keep his attention on you, even when you are not around. The reason for this is that it helps control his libido. If his libido is focused on you, his fantasies and his thoughts will be as well. No matter what else he does during the day, his thoughts will return to you and how great sex is with you. By doing this, you assure yourself that your erotic power will always be there when you want to use it.

But along with the teasing, we are going to introduce the thing that gives you the most power... Orgasm denial! When you don't allow your husband to have an orgasm he is expecting, it will ensure that his mind will remain on you. This is the ultimate use of your erotic power.

Why Denial?

Everything we have done so far has been leading up to this point. We have grabbed his attention by granting him more sex than he ever thought possible and we have gotten him (hopefully) to pay a bit more attention to your needs. But this is where we will teach him that he is NOT the one in charge.

By denying a man his orgasm (or ejaculation), we put him in the position of wanting more. He may feel cheated and get upset. He may run to the bathroom to finish what you have started. But that's okay. At least for now. It is, of course, preferable that he not relieve himself, but it won't be detrimental to what you are trying to accomplish if he does. After all, he would much rather you did it than have to finish it alone.

Handling His Behavior

If you'll recall, we mentioned earlier that, when a man ejaculates, certain chemical and physiological things happen to him. What we didn't mention is that the effects those changes can actually last for several days. That means that he will not be as easily aroused or as interested in sex as he would be if he had not ejaculated. Therefore, by controlling when, and how often he ejaculates, we can control his behavior much easier.

If you have been teasing him on a regular basis, he will have gotten used to having that really strong release (ejaculation or orgasm as we call it) at the end of each session. This is what his body has taught him should happen. We need to train his mind to understand that it's not the orgasm that is most pleasing, but the arousal before that makes sex so much fun.

In order to train his mind, you need to retrain his thought process where sexual gratification is concerned. That will take a bit of verbal reinforcement on your part. During your first tease and denial session, you should make a point of asking him if he enjoys all the teasing you have been doing. That is, make him admit that he loves it when you give his body (his penis in particular) all the attention he can stand.

Once you have gotten him to admit it, ask him precisely what it is that he enjoys the most. Coax him to tell you exactly what things that you have done to him that turned him on and make sure he tells you why. This will get his thoughts flowing in the right direction.

Having done all that, while you are teasing him, try to do the things he tells you are the most exciting. After you have teased him for a good long time (say an hour or more) tell him that when he actually ejaculates, it's kind of a let down for you. Tell him that it is because it signals the end of both your pleasure and his.

Try to get him to agree with you. After all, when he ejaculates, you will stop the teasing and he will no longer desire it. Remind him that he will probably not even want sex for awhile. Maybe even a day or two. Be sure to ask if he enjoys being turned on. There can be only one answer to that question, "Yes."

Once he agrees that what you are saying is true, he will be like putty in your hands. Simply explain to him that you would rather he wanted sex all the time. Ask him if he would like that. Whether he agrees with you or not, it's time to stop. Stop teasing him and tell him that you will let him have his orgasm the next time you tease him. Ask him not to masturbate before your next session. Tell him exactly when that session will be and keep your promise. Don't make him wait more than a day, or two at the most.

Let's examine why ejaculation should not be your goal. When a man ejaculates, certain endorphins that are released during arousal stop. Certain hormones signal the penis to stop retaining blood and his erection is lost. At least temporarily. In normal instances, it is unlikely that his desire for sexual activity will return for at least twenty-four hours, sometimes longer. Many men won't have a strong sexual desire for forty-eight hours or more. The exceptions being those men who spend a great deal of time looking at pornography. By the way, it takes six to twelve hours for his semen to regenerate to full capacity, anyway.

So by denying him his orgasm, you effectively keep him in a heightened sexual state for an extended period of time. Denial, coupled with the daily teasing I taught you in an another chapter, allows you to keep him aroused and thinking of you for as long as you want him to. It will also allow you more effective control over his attention. When you have his sexual desire at a peak, he will be much more willing to do things for you, such as taking out the garbage or even washing the dishes.

The ultimate goal of denying his orgasm is to get him to willingly help you make your relationship much better. When you both have the same goal, there is nothing you can't accomplish. The truth is, men have been been trained from puberty (through their own "wet dreams" that ejaculation is the best part of sex. That's why you have to train them to understand that they have been wrong all their adult lives.

Once they understand that arousal (or fore-play) is truly the best part about sex, it's easy to get them to join you in whatever you want to do as long as there is a promise of more arousal to come. Yes, you will be controlling him through sex. But whoever said that was a bad thing? It's not a bad thing when it is done correctly. That's why I wrote this book. To teach the average woman how to get more from their relationship through erotic power.

If you have difficulty getting him not to masturbate, then you might want to consider using a chastity device. It not only prevents masturbation, but it can also help in keeping your man aroused and thinking about you. How can that be a bad thing? After all, if he is more help around the house, more attentive to your needs (sexual and otherwise), won't that improve things to begin with?

Remember, when you deny him an orgasm for the first time, it is best to let him know it is going to happen. That way, he can prepare himself for it. Just be sure he understands why you are doing it.

Later, as he becomes more used to the idea of tease and denial, you will be able to deny him for longer periods of time. That means, you will have complete control over him until the next time you allow him an orgasm. Remember, every time you allow him to ejaculate, he will not be as attentive or obedient for at least a day, maybe longer.

After you have allowed your man to ejaculate, it's a good idea to go heavy on the daily teasing in order to get all those chemicals flowing again. I even recommend a long tease session the very next day. That way, you can shorten the period of "neglect" that may follow his orgasm.

There are games you can play as well as other systems you can use to keep him anticipating that next orgasm. If you put your mind to it, I am sure you can come up with a few on your own.

Your First T&D Session

During this first tease and denial session it's extremely important that you don't allow your partner the opportunity to ejaculate (have an orgasm). So you want to use an extremely light touch. Don't forget, if you even **think** he is getting too close to an orgasm, you MUST STOP touching him altogether for at least a minute. Bearing that in mind, here is what you should be doing.

Don't touch him firmly enough to even move the skin of your husband's penis. That is the best way to perform this type of teasing. This procedure will require that you keep his penis well lubricated. There a number of excellent lubrications on the market. KY Jelly® being the most common and the most widely used. Even KY makes several varieties, but stick to the plain stuff. No need to get fancy here. For that matter, baby oil, mineral oil, even vegetable oil will work as long as you keep everything as slippery as possible at all times during this session.

Let's face it, unless you are trying to produce an orgasm, perhaps so that you can ruin it, you don't

want to touch him with anything more than a
feather touch. The point of this type of penis tease is
to make him **want** to feel your touch more than you
are permitting. It will drive him crazy with desire for
a firmer touch. So if your goal is to tease and deny
(and it should be in this first tease session) then this
is the best way to achieve the desired results.

Remember, whether you think he is getting too close
to his orgasm or not, it doesn't hurt to take a break
every so often in order to let his desire (or
immediate need to orgasm) wane just a bit. This will
produce a great deal more precum because each
time he is re-aroused, he will (or should) produce it.

Precum, if you are not familiar with the term, is that
few drops of clear liquid that appears when a man
gets fully aroused. It is a natural lubrication
designed to aid in penetration during normal
intercourse. It is one of the most slippery lubricants
I have ever experienced, so if you can use it, do so.
By-the-way, precum has little or no taste, unlike
semen. Don't be afraid to find out for yourself, if you
like. But I digress.

During these little breaks you can fondle his balls,
his nipples, his inner-thighs, or any other part of his
body. Use your imagination, and pay attention to his
reactions to everything you do. He may just surprise
you with what turns him on at this point. Avoid
actually tickling him. This can be too much of a
distraction. You can tickle him if you think he is

getting too close to ejaculating. Sometimes that will distract him enough to stave off an ejaculation.

During this session, you can tell him one of his favorite fantasies, or have him tell it to you. You should keep the erotic talking going. If nothing else, talk about what you are doing to his penis. Ask him if it is turning him on. Tell him that are going to do something different this time, but you are not ready to tell him what it is. Tell him how exciting you find it to tease his penis the way you have been doing for the past few weeks. Ask him if he is happy with all the attention he has been getting. Ask him to perform some task that he normally does not do, such as wash the dishes for you. If he agrees, go back to talking about things that turn him on.

Don't be surprised if you accidentally go too far. If that happens and he begins to show the signs of an impending orgasm, simply stop touching him. Allow him time to rest for at least a full minute before continuing. He may actually have, what we call, a "ruined" orgasm. A ruined orgasm is one that does not contain the full force of a 'normal' orgasm (or ejaculation). It means that he is not fully satisfied and he will not experience the usual let down. That is, it does NOT mean the end of his arousal. Most men are capable of having several ruined orgasms in one session, but only one full orgasm.

If this happens, don't be alarmed. Don't get upset. You can continue with the tease session as long as he does not have a full orgasm. You can assume it was not a full orgasm if it does not shoot out as it normally would. You should have had enough practice by this point to recognize what his 'normal', full orgasms are like.

As I said, take a minute, every now and then, to fondle other parts of his body. Rub or pinch his nipples. Fondle his balls with one or both hands. Tickle the insides of his thighs with your fingernails. Run the flat of your hands down his chest and stomach to his thighs. All of these things and more can be erotic to your partner. Don't be afraid to experiment. Find out what he likes and do it while taking short breaks from stroking his penis. It will make him last longer, and it will give you a way to keep him aroused while not stimulating him too much.

Remember what I told you before. The whole point of this session is to tease his penis for as long as you can while talking to him about sexual desire. In this session, you should be aiming toward convincing him that not having an orgasm is a good thing. If you can spend an hour or more teasing his penis like this, then you should have no trouble getting him to ask you (even beg you) for anything you want. Many women love to make their men beg for things. Things like, a full orgasm, the chance to earn one by doing the dishes for a full week. Just about anything you can think of can be the object of his begging. Just because he begs you to let him do something, doesn't mean that you have to let him do it. For example, he may beg you to allow him an orgasm if he washes the dishes every night for a week. Remember, you are in charge of his orgasms (or you should be by now). You can always find a reason NOT to let him have his orgasm. It's always best to make him perform his part of the bargain first. So if your deal is to allow a full orgasm in exchange for a week of dish washing, make him wait until he has washed the dishes for a week before giving him that orgasm.

Once he sees your point about ejaculation marking the end of a sexual encounter, it should be a simple thing to get him to agree that you should not allow him an orgasm this one time. Just to try it out. (That's what you tell him, anyway.) If he agrees, make him promise not to masturbate before your next session. Make it very clear exactly when that session will be so that he understands just how long he will have to abstain.

Once he actually agrees to all this, stop. Don't touch him again. Get up. Tell him that you want him to stay aroused until the next time and that you are going to help him do just that. (That's what all the daily teasing is for.)

The hard part is making him wait. If he has a tendency to masturbate, assure him that he won't have to wait too long. Don't make him wait more than a day or two or he will, most likely, masturbate and ruin your plans. If he can be trusted not to take care of it himself, then you can make him wait a little longer. But you have to make sure he is NOT neglected during this time by making use of daily teasing. You want to show him that you will keep your end of the bargain and help him to stay aroused at least most of the time.

From this point on, you have control of his orgasms. He will ejaculate only when you allow it. You might want to read the chapter on chastity. If he has a tendency to masturbate, you might want to limit his opportunities to do so. Forbid him to go to his favorite Internet sites. Remove any magazines he might be using for masturbation. Keep him too busy to do it. If he can't find the time, he will be more likely to abstain.

In future sessions, whether you tease and deny or allow him a full orgasm is up to you. You should continue to have a full session at least once a week, two would be better. In fact, the more often you tease him the stronger your erotic power over him will be.

Making Your Fantasies Come True

Control! That's what it's all about. Taking control of your relationship, of your sex life, of him. That's what this chapter is all about. So pay close attention.

Okay, by now you have had several teasing sessions that ended with him having a full orgasm. You have learned to talk freely, and to talk "dirty" during sex (hopefully). You have even denied him an orgasm (or two, or three). And, hopefully, you have started using little daily teases to keep him aroused between those long tease and denial sessions. So what's next?

If you have done everything I have suggested so far, all you need to do now is take control. Actually, you have already taken control of your sex lives, both yours and his. But the over all goal of improving your relationship is not, yet, complete. Now you need to take control of all of his activities. You want him to do more to help out around the house. Right? You also want him to take you out on dates like he did when he was courting you. Right? Well then, it's time you put all that erotic power you have to work.

Remember that list of things you would like him to do around the house.? It should include things like taking you to dinner or out to see that new chick-flick you have been wanting to see. Introduce the list one thing at a time. Perhaps you could ask him to start doing the dishes for you every night. Ask him with a suggestion of earning an orgasm if he does it. Use the same method to get him to do one or two other things on your list.

Keep score! I don't care how you do it, but you need to keep a record of all the things you have asked him to that he hasn't done. Maybe he only did the dishes for five nights instead of the required seven. Or maybe he forgot to take you to a movie, or to help your children with their homework. This would be a good time to set up a merit system so that you can keep track of his behavior.

Once you have accomplished that, wait for your next tease sessions. Then present him with a short list of things you want him to do on a regular basis. Present the list during your tease session. You might need to promise him a full orgasm if he does all those things without complaining. Don't wait too long to give him that orgasm. After all, you want positive reinforcement of his behavior, assuming, of course, that he has done the things you asked.

If you keep adding a few things at a time to your list of chores for him to do, you should, very soon, have him happily doing all the things you have always wanted him to do. This is when you are ready to set up a merit system for him.

In a merit system, you don't take points away if he forgets (or just fails) to do something. Instead, you give him points for the things that he **does** accomplish. Set a goal for him. Say, once he earns 'X' number of points you will give him an orgasm. That way, it's on him if he fails to please you. If it takes him a month to earn enough points to receive an orgasm, then maybe he should work harder to earn one sooner. Just make sure it's all on him. That way, you are not the 'bad guy' for holding him back, he is.

It is always better to use a merit system as opposed to a demerit system simply because you want to reward his good behavior, not punish his bad behavior. In other words, you are going to reward him with sexual "favors" when he does what you want him to.

You can use any method you like, for example; You could make a list of the chores he is to perform during the week. If he does enough of them (without complaint), then he gets to have an orgasm on the weekend. Otherwise, he will have to wait another week or suffer a ruined orgasm. It's up to you how you reward him, just make sure it's done consistently. If you are consistent, he will be as well.

You can actually come up with some rewards on your own, like, allowing him to watch the game on Sunday afternoon. Or maybe choosing the movie the next time you go out. It's up to you what you use as a reward, but the overall punishment for failure should be the withholding of sexual release. Remember, if he masturbates between sessions, he will destroy everything you have worked for. In other words, he will be taking away some of your erotic power. We just can't have that, now can we?

Two of the women whose success stories I have included in this book have set up what they call a "30 Day" program. Here's how it works. If her husband behaves himself, does the chores he has been assigned, and treats her the way she wants he can earn a day toward an orgasm. He must earn thirty days in order for her to allow the orgasm.

It may be rare for him to get his orgasm in thirty days since he often loses days by not doing as he is expected. If he fails to earn a day, it will take him that much longer to earn the thirty he needs. According to her, he very rarely gets his orgasm in thirty days. But, over time, he has gotten much better at earning his days as he should.

As I said, you can use whatever system you like and provide whatever rewards you think will help. I would suggest using a merit system with more than one reward attached. For example, he must earn his thirty days as in the example above, but if he gets six days in a row, he can watch whatever game he likes to watch on the weekend. That way, you can give small rewards for at least attempting to behave, even if he doesn't get the 'big' reward, yet. You might even break it down into smaller increments, such as, if he does well one day, he can have an extra fifteen minutes of teasing that night at bedtime, or he will be allowed to please you that night instead.

These are only suggestions and you are, of course free to use whatever system of rewards you like. Men seem to respond well to earning things they like, so find out what those are and use them. Perhaps he would be more responsive to some kind of game of chance for his rewards. You could use dice, cards, chips, or even a roulette wheel to make the determination as to what reward he earns. For example, each successful day he has he is allowed to draw one card from a deck of fifty-two. If he gets an ace, he can have an orgasm. If he gets a face card, he gets so many minutes of tease-time that night. Any other card gets him nothing.

That's just one example of ways you can use to keep your man interested and playing the 'game' of good behavior for orgasms. I am sure you can come up with others that will suit your specific needs. Just remember, a man's behavior immediately after an orgasm, and for the next few days, may not be ideal. That's why we make it difficult (but not impossible) for him to earn an orgasm.

What About Chastity?

Why are we even talking about chastity? Remember when I told you masturbation was the enemy of erotic power? Well, chastity is important. If your husband cannot refrain from masturbating without your permission, then he will be taking away your power to control him. Therefore, chastity is important. If he cannot refrain from masturbating, you will need to discuss using a male chastity device to help him control his bad habit.

Chastity is a personal thing. Whether or not you choose to use a chastity device or not is up to you. I DO NOT recommend forcing your partner into wearing a chastity device of any kind. This will only cause you both problems. It must be agreed to by both parties if it is to be successful.

There are two basic forms of chastity: 1) The honor system used by monks around the world as well as various priests; and 2) Use of a chastity device which, in most cases, guarantees chastity will be maintained.

It should be obvious that maintaining chastity between sessions is extremely important. Even though a chastity device can be a great way to accomplish that, it may not be desirable, or even necessary.

Male chastity has become a very popular 'kink' these days. You can now purchase a chastity device at your local sex store, not to mention every adult toy store on line. But just because it is popular is no reason to jump on the band wagon. There are as many reasons to use a chastity device as there are reasons not to. You should talk it over with your husband before running out and purchasing your first chastity device. You might find that he may jump at the chance to wear such a device just as a sexual reminder of you. On the other hand, he may not.

Perhaps your partner feels too uncomfortable. Maybe the device you have chosen does not really fit as well as either of you would like. Of course, you could have one custom made, but even then, you may have problems. Let's face it, male chastity (in its popular form) is a fairly recent addition to the kink scene. Yet, many strides have been made, making it a viable alternative to the honor system.

There are literally thousands of stories on the Internet about women who have put their man (or men) in chastity and have kept them that way for years at a time. Though there may be a few who actually have, they are very rare. My point is, male chastity is so new to the scene that it is highly unlikely that more than a handful of couples have been into it that deeply. The past ten years have witnessed a huge growth in male chastity. Before that, very few people actually practiced it at all.

The truth about male chastity is that many couples only practice it occasionally for relatively short periods of time. Male chastity is like any other kink, it's fun for awhile, but if you practice it constantly for years at a time, chances are the thrill will fade and the enjoyment could vanish altogether. If it turns boring, no one will want to do it.

It is my opinion that many couples would do better using tease and denial techniques to keep their sex lives interesting. Although male chastity is often a big part of tease and denial, it is by no means necessary. Even if you have one of those partners who will masturbate in private when he has been denied an ejaculation or two, that is no reason that you have to run right out and spend a couple hundred bucks on a chastity device.

There can be enough pleasure (hopefully for the both of you) in teasing that even the denial does not have to be an integral part of your play. More often than not, when a woman enjoys teasing her partner's penis (at least physically), she will extend her play far longer than would ever happen in a standard love-making session. After all, teasing can be great fun for both partners. So whether you incorporate denial, much less chastity, in your play, chances are you will both be more satisfied. Isn't that the point of teasing in the first place?

So whether or not you choose to engage in male chastity, tease and denial can help improve your sexual enjoyment. So, the use of a chastity device on your partner is simply a matter of choice. It is something you should discuss in depth, both the pro's and the con's, before jumping right in. I suggest, if you are interested in male chastity, start out slowly and as inexpensively as you can.

For more information on male chastity and chastity devices, I suggest using your favorite search engine on the Internet. There is plenty of information out there, but I would caution you to be mindful of some of the stories you may read. Remember, they are just stories and like the movies we all love to watch, anything can happen. Even things that are not physically possible in real life.

Having said all that, should you choose to use a chastity device, punishment for masturbation should no longer be necessary. On the other hand, teasing your partner sexually while he is wearing such a device can be great fun. After all, he knows there is no way he is going to have an orgasm while in chastity. So to promote good behavior, you can promise to remove it the next time you tease him (if he earns enough merits).

Many men actually enjoy being placed in physical chastity. So it is something that you might want to talk to your partner about. I would also recommend that you have a written agreement if you choose to use a device to maintain chastity. I have included a brief outline of what should be included in such an agreement below.

1. Definitions of any terms used in the agreement that could be misinterpreted.

2. Things expected of the wearer of the device:

   a. How long it will be warn.

   b. When it will be removed for such things as:

      - cleaning

      - teasing

      - travel

   c. What chores etc., will be required of him.

   d. When or how often he can expect to be allowed an orgasm.

   e. Any other rules that will be imposed on the wearer.

3. Things expected of the key holder (woman in charge).

   a. Where an emergency key can be found.

   b. What kinds of teasing and how often she will provide it.

   c. What limits she will allow him to have. Etc.

Anything else that you might find important should also be included in your agreement. Both parties should be allowed to negotiate what goes into the agreement while on equal terms. That is, while he is NOT wearing the device.

If this basic outline is used, and both parties have a say in what goes into the agreement, everything should go smoothly. You can always make changes to your agreement as time goes by and things change.

Here are a few things that you might like to know about the basic chastity devices on the market. I won't go into detail about any specific brands because I do not want to get into that. But, here are the basics...

Male chastity devices are made of one of three basic materials: plastic, metal, or silicone. Each has its own set of pro's and con's. Any good chastity device should have the ability to have a locking mechanism (a small lock) attached to it to prevent unwanted removal.

Some wearers have complained that certain models can be, at least partially, removed. It is often called "pulling out." What happens is that the wearer is able to pull his penis (but not his testicles) out the back of the device and, therefore, can masturbate at will. Most of these are very difficult to replace the penis back into the device and, as such, the wearer often gets caught. Some of the devices on the market include "pull out" restraints designed to prevent the wearer from pulling his penis free. I cannot attest to the effectiveness of these devices, but I am told they work very well.

Another feature of certain chastity devices is something called "spikes." They are normally an add-on feature. Spikes are designed to prevent the penis from achieving any kind or erection while in the chastity device. Most work very well. They cause a certain amount of pain whenever the wearer begins to get aroused. I have tried some of these devices and they do work, though the unaroused size of the wearer's penis effects how much arousal he can take before the pain gets to be too much.

There are several companies who manufacture custom fitted devices. Some of those are full belts while others are only the genital confinement style. You can expect to pay several hundred dollars for any custom device. Again, the choice is yours. But I do recommend that you do your research before you invest a dime in any male chastity device.

Success Stories

Here a few letters from friends who have been successful at creating female lead relationships. Notice, if you will, what they all have in common as well as the things they do differently. It is these success stories (and others like them), along with my own successful relationship that lead me to create this book in the first place. But I have said enough. I'll let the letters speak for themselves. (By-the-way, 'Mistress Ivey' is my Internet handle. So if you are looking for me, try using that in your favorite search engine.)

Dear Mistress Ivey:

My husband James and I have been married for over 20 years and are both in our mid 40's with three teen children. I was introduced to the concept of a chastity relationship and that of male chastity devices from my sister in law. I then introduced this to my husband. I did this in a series of provocative steps by teasing my husband and then approached him on chastity as a sex toy and game and it then became a fantasy of his. We have been practicing a chastity relationship now for about 2 years.

We initially decided to start using a device simply as a means to spice up a stale, anemic sex life - one that became infrequent and with no feeling or spark. From the get-go our sex life improved quite dramatically. As James started wearing the device the first thing that became clear that part of the source of our anemic sex life was that he had been doing a lot of daily masturbation in the shower. Once this was stopped he had considerable additional energy. Once we began to play in this manner our relationship also began to change as we developed increased intimacy. For me intimacy-thoughts and feelings are the real reasons to why we do this. Isn't intimacy the true goal of being a couple and the lack of intimacy over time being why many couples drift apart and separate?

In my experience opening the communication channels is what started the intimacy process. Firstly James needed to learn to listen better. He never really wanted to before. As things progressed with our incorporation of chastity devices, and to make things more interesting we defined formal rules such that my husband needed to earn his way out with 30 "earned" days. James had to fulfill duties in areas of the home, family and especially personal service to me.

I think that this system enhanced James's listening skills as he began to listen much more as he had to be able to keep me satisfied enough to give him an "earned day". As he listened more along came his increased ability to understand and communicate - to relate to both his and to my inner feelings. Once he started to really listen he began to really understand thoughts and feelings and then we took it to another level - his ability to openly and honestly express his inner self to me. More importantly this encouraged me to open up even more to him and the bonds between us got even much closer.

The chastity device was the tool that enabled me to make all of this to happen. The problem I think with most men is that they sometimes need to be pried open. The chastity device helps this out. If they resist then it just takes longer for them to come around but the key-holder can have them wait as long as it takes until this happens. Men can also justify to themselves that the device was the reason that they made the changes - thus there is a scapegoat for their mind.

Once we began initially to play in this manner our relationship also began to change in other ways. As the key holder I found that I began to assert my expectations into other areas. I was able to encourage James to become much more of a meaningful family role model and he now demonstrates to our girls on how a husband and father should act. Previously, in my opinion, we were not a terribly functional family.

Once I became the key holder and became comfortable with this role I saw the possibilities and ran with them. As James began to do more of what I "asked" his respect began to show through and my self-pride was reinforced. I also insisted that part of James's responsibility (to earn days) be with closer attention and focus on the family. I essentially forced James to reinforce his roles as both a husband and father.

The girls began to see a self-confident mother with a husband who respected her and tried to do as she expected and they also began to see a father who cared and was there to support and guide them. They don't quite understand how we changed but they know that we made an effort to strengthen our relationship because we wanted to improve our love for each other and for them. They have responded very positively and are learning the possibilities for what a marriage and family can be.

The chastity device has really enabled me to guide James to open up and expand all of our bonds. Although we are straight in front of them they do see from me that a woman should take pride in herself and also expect for her wishes to be met. We are both ok with my being more assertive as it still seems as though this extension in my authority is related to our chastity play in earning days to get out. We have both accepted this as the necessity of practicing chastity. On major areas such as decisions with the children or on financial matters we consider ourselves to be equal decision makers. In order to enforce the system, I devised demerits. James receives a demerit when he does something of a negative nature. Two demerits lead to a lost day but 4 in a two-week period lead to a lost week. When I actually reviewed the demerits over time of the last year (being an accountant by profession, I look at numerical details) I found something quite surprising. James received 93% of all of his demerits in the first 14 days from each last orgasm. Looking further he got 78% of all his demerits in the first 7 days from each last orgasm. Only 7% of all demerits were received in the last 16+ days until next orgasm. No demerits have ever occurred in the last week to next orgasm. I had always noticed that within the first week James's attention and feelings to me were suppressed and I had seen how much more intimate he became after this first week but looking at the demerit data suggests how much the longer durations in chastity effect the entire scheme of things. I am quite sure that it has got to be the hormones. James's release dates can vary significantly from 30 earned days. He has been locked up for as long as about 48 days (6 demerits in a two week span) but now usually gets out in about 30-35 day periods - a combination of failing to earn days with a few demerits thrown in. Assigning demerits as I see fit keeps James more focused and on his toes then if he had a list and also this is part of the tease. Naturally, begging for releases incurs demerits and so James doesn't do that at all now.

Initially the device was just a great plastic toy (CB3000) - off more than on. My husband is now using an open bar stainless metal device as the plastic device cracked at the seam. Since he doesn't have a piercing, he wears a stainless steel belt that attaches to his device so that he cannot pull out of the back of the device. The device is quite easy to keep clean and since he gets out regularly (about 30 day intervals) he seems quite healthy in his performance.

I also began to have fun teasing him while he was locked as this keeps us close. When we are not in the bedroom, I use frequent good reminders and reinforcement of his condition. You must remember that we have 3 teen-aged girls who are quite perceptive so direct teasing is subdued around them. However this in itself adds to the tease. Also in passing I might brush past James with a light touch to a sensitive area. I also wear the key to the device on a necklace (with other stones) and it rests between my breasts and so pulling it up and fiddling with it under James's watchful eye (sometimes with other people around) then putting it back properly has quite an effect.

In the bedroom I like to stroke and rub the cage while reviewing days remaining. We focus on my pleasure and what would be good for my present mood. I also like oral and I frequently prefer a strap-on dildo that fits to his cage. These actions keep him quite frustrated and on the edge.

The trick of the tease with the dildo attached to the device (for me) starts when I put it on him while I tell him how much fun it will be for both of us. I massage his cage and rub him with fingers and nails tapping and scratching and sometimes with the tongue then slowly put the dildo on over the cage. He gets so frustrated and it makes him even more aroused afterward. Unless he is going to be released I do not usually remove his cage as he has a hair trigger. This keeps mistakes to a minimum.

Anticipation leading up to a release is more of the event for both of us then the actual. When he does get out it is such a fantastic and joyous time for both of us. I also like personal attentions such as to be dried off after a bath or shower. Since we switched to an open cage device it is easy for both of us to inspect everything and for James to clean everyday - thus no reason to remove the cage for cleaning.

We do live a normal life and are quite vanilla. To be honest I don't see us as kinky. I suppose if we were more into classical BDSM we might be. I don't think that chastity devices themselves are the defining point for kink. It is what else one does that is.

I am a manager (to several men and women) in my job and quite assertive and so the role of being dominant doesn't seem to be uncomfortable at all. To me being assertive was learned as in my professional development. I just wasn't dominant at home until the advent of the chastity device with my husband. Up to that point we considered ourselves to be equal team members - as many modern marriages seem to be today.

Looking back I would state that it was my sister-in-law who really framed chastity to me as a form of relationship builder but suggested that it needed to be approached to James as a sex game. The point that came out to me was that the woman is really the guiding force in building an improved relationship and that chastity simply is a tool to reinforce the man to be guided. However it needs to be sold to the man in terms of fantasy play and sex games. Isn't this really like giving children medicine - it tastes good but has a beneficial effect. As you pointed out that the tease is really the way to approach chastity and to maintain interest in it.

Signed: Karen

Dear Mistress Ivey;

My wife Gail and I have a FLR [Female Led Relationship], but not in a conventional sense. We consider ourselves to be equals in all areas but the bedroom. The truth is that this is a FLR, but not in an overt way. Aside from a couple of indulgences (fast food and fast cars) pretty much everything that I do is for keeping Gail happy and provided for. Such is the life of a husband and father.

We have been together for 14 years, and married for 13, and have never had an argument. That speaks more towards compatibility and patience than dominance and submission. We have both been divorced twice and third time lucky. Thanks to some good counseling, I have been able to submit to my wife in the biblical sense. Most men say they would die for their mate - I have learned to live for her.

We do have a couple of major differences: one is that she is a morning person, and generally dead to the world after 9P.M. My clock is in a different time zone. The other difference is that our sex drives are miles apart. She came from a conservative, "churchy" background which will either turn you into a slut or a prude. Let's just say that I have had to introduce her to my world on a gradual basis.

My first awareness of my kink dates back to getting a bit of a buzz over Mrs. Emma Peale's leather cat-suits and occasional bondage predicaments on the old 'Avenger's' television show from the early 60's. I used to enjoy getting captured by the girls while playing at recess. My 3 older brothers had an extensive magazine selection during the late 60's and early 70's when liberal thought was this was a healthy means of expression. I was particularly drawn to any portrayal that involved bondage. Interestingly, my dad's porn stash generally consisted of magazines that had pictures of bondage. (Nature, or nurture?)

Through the years I have given Gail gifts of leather lingerie and even whips in the hope of sparking a dominant sexual awakening- or even a bit more interest in sex. We had played with B&D, and some role playing, but unless all conditions were exactly right, not much worked. Trying to find different ways with no success was starting to wear on me. In the fall of '08, temptation reared its head. Through the course of my job I encountered a young lady who had a number of attractive traits: beautiful, fit, self sufficient, and MECHANICAL ability. I knew that my chances with her were slim, but I thought through the scenarios way too much for comfort. Something had to change.

I had been trolling through the [adult toys] website[s] for interesting gear when I discovered a page for chastity devices. At first, this appealed mostly to my kinky side - especially after reading the 'testimonials', but then I began to look with new purpose. I sat down with Gail for a heart to heart talk. I told her of my temptation, and the frustration I was feeling about our sexual relationship. I was at wits end of trying to light a fire within her, but that I was willing to try a means to dial back my sexual drive. She looked at the web page with me, and I steered her towards the CB 6000 chastity device. The price was reasonable, and the aesthetics were less objectionable than the other devices.

Thinking back, I think that her consent was more a matter of indulging me and my kink as a diversionary tactic. I wasn't satisfied with just being accommodated. I went back to the computer to do more research. I found [another good] website and devoured it. Aside from the great wanking material, I followed a link to [another] website. A couple of the testimonials had the information that Gail needed to see. I got her to read them, and while she couldn't see herself going as far, she was finally able to understand what I needed, and how it could benefit her. She finally agreed to be my key-holder. You could call it topping from the bottom, but I continued to find websites and share bits of information to help lead Gail in the right direction.

Through this learning and growing process, Gail has seen her dominant side rise closer to the surface. She values her opinion more around the home, and has more confidence and assertiveness at work. The thought that she wears the key to my cage around her neck is our joke on the world. She is learning the art of tease and denial, and at times can be quite good at it. Every so often she even gives me the pleasure of seeing her dressed from head to toe in black leather as my whip dragging dominatrix. Then she usually blindfolds me. You get the picture. Life is good.

Barring equipment failure, and the odd rash or spot, I have been locked up pretty much continuously since the first CB6000 arrived in Nov. '08. We tried playing the release games, and decided it was BS and wasn't true submission. I am 'permanently' locked up - she simply wouldn't have it any other way. My favorite sexual position is kneeling at the edge of the bed between my queen's legs.
My chastity devices feel like more of a symbol of commitment than my wedding ring ever did. They are something of a constant reminder of that deeper commitment that sexual submission is. You don't forget you are wearing one. Since my thing isn't about escape, I am not concerned that the devices we have aren't escape proof and only prevent ejaculation unless you are absolutely determined. Commitment and integrity play an important role. But sometimes, the spirit was willing, but the flesh was weak. There are times too, when the sub in me just needs a good beating.

They say that indulging your fantasies is the slippery slope on the road to hell. It is all about balance. Sometimes a chastity device and a little T&D is the best way to equalize our differences, be they strengths or weakness. Life is about learning and growing. As Gene Simmons says: "Sometimes, it's good to be... me." Couldn't agree more.

Signed: Jeff

Dear Mistress Ivey;

I met my husband Brad while in college. After graduation we got married and raised 2 boys - who are themselves now in college. Although Brad and I are very much in love we have had issues over the past years but have very much always wanted to remain as a couple. I would have to say that Brad and I are both fairly assertive people. Brad has a "know it all" personality, can be quite aggressive, doesn't listen and is downright rude on occasions - although he is so definitive and confident that people tend to follow his thoughts with little question.

After our kids left for college several years ago, Brad's personality actions tended to bother me much more and I wanted to make changes. This was due to a combination of not having the distraction of the kids to buffer things but also because of Brad's work success he tended to get much more assertive over time. At one point I also suspected that Brad may have had a brief interlude although that later proved not to be the case. Never the less I wanted to put a stop to what I thought was a possibility.

During this period I looked at many options including those on the web and came upon a site that involved alternate lifestyles. The one on chastity control seemed to "fill the bill".

It reminded me of the sign that one of President Nixon's cabinet members once had in his office "When you've got them by the balls their hearts and minds will follow."

I wrote a note to a woman seeking advice on how to get started and she put me in touch with a knowledgeable woman "coach." Her name was Jane and she lives in England. After much correspondence we set up a plan that involved a set of goals and milestones that would encompass at least a year to accomplish. Jane had never worked with an alpha male and so was cautious with much doubt on a successful outcome.

Essentially the plan was as follows;

1. Begin to dress more provocatively including leather mini skirts.

2. Introduce the concept of me taking control in the bedroom to spice things up.

3. Expand to sex toys and then migrate to a simple plastic chastity device (CB3000).

4. In an effort to make the experience more real - expand the commitment to more permanent and secure metal equipment. Jane always recommended a belt for its security.

5. Once the equipment was permanent and secure, training of Brad's behavior problems could then (and only then) be attempted.

The idea was to work slowly and draw Brad into either suggesting each next step or agreeing because it seemed either logical or exciting to try. We had many trials and tribulations along the way. However slightly past one year we completed our plan.

As we migrated to metal I decided that a [all steel] belt was too hard to sell to Brad but thought that another brand of steel belt would work as they allowed it to work with a CB3000. Brad was okay with this as it was still being attached to plastic. Later I worked with [another company] to allow one of [their] devices to attach to the belt. [Their] devices mostly require piercing but with the belt Jane and I felt that it was quite secure (proved correct). I knew that Brad would never go for a piercing and these all needed to be gradual changes. At this stage Jane felt that her work was completed and further training was up to me.

[A friend] suggested placing Brad on a 30 earned day regimen to keep him motivated. He needs to please me, never offend me and also do more house chores to earn a day. She also advised that I needed to show him that I meant business and so I had both an old horse riding quirt (from my high school times) and a (purchased) paddle on hand. I should add that Brad's belt comes with a D ring on either side in the front for wrist restraints and we also have a panel gag that allows use of the tools with mostly silence. After several uses with the tools and expanded durations of chastity Brad became motivated to earn days toward release and I was then able to take charge and correct the issues I wanted (and did).

Since then our relationship is really so much more close and we are both very happy. Brad now admits that this has been a good experience and that both he and I are better people for doing this.

Our relations involve much oral sex and use of a dildo that attaches to his device. Unless released for intercourse, I unlock Brad (with wrist restraints) and usually tease him with feathers, my tongue and, often, strokes to his penis. I pretty much know how far to take things. I have also used Bengay®. This happens about 3 days each week. He usually gets out for full intercourse on a 30-day period as he now seldom loses days. When he is released there are no restraints and it is usually an exciting evening - sometimes extending over for more than one evening.

Signed: Sara

Dear Mistress Ivey;

I am in my 50's, and have lived all but one year thinking, living, and embracing 'vanilla' thoughts. So how did I end up where I am, waking up in the morning, getting her shower ready, draping a towel and washcloth over the shower curtain rod, putting her deodorant on the sink counter and toothpaste on her brush all before she sets her feet to the floor and begins her day? While she's showering I make the bed, tidy the room, feed the cats, check her email, get her vitamins and meds out along with a glass of water, and hustle back upstairs ready to blow dry and comb her hair. Why did I decide to make her thoughts and needs my foremost priority? What changed that made me want to do chores for her, that caused me to want to give all of my thoughts, energy, effort, and desire to her, so much so that I now think of me second, making her my foremost priority - and actually enjoy doing all of this?

To be perfectly honest, it happened totally by chance. One day I was reading a story a woman wrote and posted on an adult online web page. In that story, she told how she came to dominate her man sexually. When I read it, it triggered quite the unexpected reaction within. I liked it. In fact, I loved it. That story had links to other similar ones and I spent many hours over several days reading about other women dominating men - mostly in ways I cared not to ever experience myself. The stories spoke about women controlling men, and being pleased by them sexually. The depicted men loving being treated this way and loving the sexual service they rendered at the whim of the women that controlled them. Some men were publicly humiliated, others blackmailed, others were 'found out' by their wives and others simply asked it they could submit themselves to the authority of a woman - to serve as their sub. What was a sub? I had never heard of that term before. What was it that excited me so much? There was something in those stories that peaked my interest and I set out to find what it was.

Being the type of person I am I hit the web running, engulfing everything I could find. I learned about professional Dominatrix's, about service-oriented submissives, about men dressing as women and doing the housework in a blouse and skirt, about men (and women) serving as slaves to their Dominant partner. I realized there were Master's and Mistresses out there and lots and lots of men desiring to be dominated by a woman - some married, some not; some being dominated via the internet and paying for the privilege of being dominated by a woman living hundreds of miles away - one they'd only seen on a web-cam. There was something about this whole lifestyle that appealed to me. It was like nothing I had ever thought of before. It was so radically different from how I had lived. It was something that I wanted to try.

I had ended a marriage of many years and was dating another woman that I had fallen love with. She too had come from a normal heterosexual relationship of many years. We were both Christians, both raised as you probably were - in a male lead home. We had both married and both perpetuated that traditional lifestyle, instilling traditional family values into our own children along the way. When I met and got to know my girl, one of her attracting qualities was her openness. I could talk to her about anything and so I broached the subject about FLR after reading lots. We talked. Surprisingly she identified somewhat with the topic of women being the head of the home. She reflected on her former marriage and how she felt in many ways she was that person - not a Dominant - but the head of her home. She shared with me how she was the one that took care of the finances, raised and instilled values into her kids, ran the home, planned the meals, interacted with other women planning social events, made decisions with respect upkeep at home, making major purchases, deciding on where they would vacation, and so much more. No, she wasn't the one bringing home the money but she was the one making all the important decisions. She was the one in charge in so many ways.

As we talked, I could identify with her. I realized that she lead the life of a dominant in so many ways. No, she wasn't being served but she was the point-person, the glue that held her marriage and family together, the one that her family came to for counsel. We had many conversations talking about female authority and during those talks she agreed that in many ways, women were better suited to lead relationships and gave good reasoning why.

Eventually I approached the 'sexual' aspect of female domination and discussed the stories I had read. We conversed mostly via email about this and it was there that I spoke more specifically about what I had read. I got the courage, wanting to know her thoughts about a woman controlling the bedroom and sent her a short email with a link to the story I had read. All I said was, "This is me. Is this you?" She responded, "This is me." Wow! She was into this. I couldn't believe it. And so we continued talking.

To be honest, what enticed me about dominance and submission was the sexual domination of the woman. I wasn't into serving her outside the bedroom anymore than most men are, but I sure wanted to experience her taking charge of me in the bedroom. I even went so far as to write and publish on-line stories about my fantasies - they were titillating and mentally drew me further into the whole D/s scene. Finally I asked her if she would consider a relationship in which she assumed the 'head' and I the submissive role. In her quiet, unassuming manner, she agreed to do so - but only on a trial basis. Yes!!!

Not knowing how to act now, I filled my perceived role of the male, based on what I had read. I walked around the house naked most of the time, I kept my eyes lowered, I tried to do everything I could for her, and I asked if I could please her sexually throughout the day. She let me do my thing but I could tell that she was not into this nearly the way I was and to be honest addressing her as 'Mistress' rather than by her name was really not me. But I did so because that was how I thought a sub should address his superior. After all, that's what everyone wrote about.

Some weeks later, I came across a fetish website and joined it. There I conversed with other submissives and slaves as well as Dommes. I wrote many dominants and asked lots of questions. I wanted to learn first-hand from those that knew the ropes. Some responded. Many didn't. However, the few that answered my questions with thought helped me immensely. One in particular conversed with me for a few weeks and she was so instrumental in helping me learn the real truth about the D/s lifestyle from a service oriented perspective. It was through her that I learned that submission wasn't just about sex but about a lifestyle of taking care of my dominant partner.

Through her, my eyes were opened still further and I began to see the magnitude of what it was I was considering - and I liked it. I struggled with this, slowly grasping how much my life could or would change. I struggled with D/s and how it meshed with my faith but rationalized that the two were able to coincide (a topic for another time). My partner and I discussed a deeper commitment and we gave each other rings signifying that commitment to one another as Domme and submissive. I made promises to submit and she told me [about] her expectations. I stopped calling her Mistress and stopped with all all the role-playing that just wasn't me. How nice it was to just focus on serving and not acting. I served [her] mostly in little ways - being the perfect gentlemen, showing lots of affection, helping her in small ways around the home, doting on her when in public, and letting her make decisions.

A few months later I ordered [a] book and read with interest a new view of service oriented submission. Most was a reiteration of the conversations I had with the dominant woman that I had been emailing but in reading [the] book, I realized more clearly what 'service' oriented submission entailed. It wasn't that she was telling me anything new, but I think I was able to reflect on her words now with a different perspective. I wasn't hearing it all for the first time and I could now digest more than initially.

Wow! When I read about what her husband did it hit me like a bomb. He prepared ALL of the meals. He ironed ALL of the clothes. He waited for her to leave a meeting or commitment. For me, it was these kinds of statements that blew me away. I swallowed hard and wondered - do I want to offer to do that for her? I couldn't. I offered to wash and dry and fold clothes. I offered to help prepare meals and clean up. But I couldn't go there fully. Yet after a month or so of 'helping' with those chores, I decided I did indeed want to serve in that way. It took me time to adjust; to understand that it really wasn't that much more work to do it all than to do most of it. And besides - I knew it would make her happy. So I asked, "Can I prepare all of your meals?" and "Can I iron your clothes?" She happily agreed. And that is where I am now.

I am learning. This is still so new. It's a process but what I can tell you is this - my initial view of submission was way off base. It was 'scene-based'. It was predicated on what I had read. It was about me, not about her. What I've learned - and am still learning - is that it's not about me. I still don't get that fully and at times pout when I don't get what I want. But at least now I realize what I'm doing and can step back and see the error of my ways. I'm taking steps into submission. Our relationship as a couple that is dating and not married limits my submission to some degree. I am certain that once we marry, my submission to her will deepen. As my love for her grows, my submission will deepen. It's a life I look forward to. I love where I am. I love where she is.

I hope my story helps you, if you are new to this or considering this lifestyle to realize that submission is work. It's hard. It takes discipline. But when you think about it - it's really about loving your partner unconditionally. It's about being selfless rather than selfish. It's about looking outward to her, rather than inward to you. It's about giving rather than getting. And the reward in doing all of this far outweighs the work. To feel the love of the one you love - well, why wouldn't every man live this way if he truly says he loves her? Submission is love in action and as the good book says, it is better to give than to receive.

Signed: Ken

How to Approach Your Wife

If you are a man who has often dreamed about having a wife who will take control of you and your sex-life, then this chapter is for you. Have you ever wanted your wife to give you more sex? Have you read stories about women who totally control their men and longed for your wife to become one of them? Have you wanted to approach your wife about a Female Lead Relationship but didn't know how? Then read on...

It is not uncommon for a man to want his wife to take control of all or just part of his marriage. Especially if he thinks he might enjoy sex more. The problem most of these men face is the fear of rejection. What if she thinks I am too kinky? What if she calls me perverted? What if she just laughs in my face? These are legitimate fears. You are not alone.

The best way to approach your spouse about an FLR is to sit down and talk about it. I understand that this can be very intimidating, but if you don't ever talk about it, I guarantee it will never happen. So you are just going to have to take a chance.

You need a plan. You need to make a list of all the reasons that you want her to take charge. Then you need a list of the ways in which an FLR would benefit her. And finally, you need a list of things that you want to do for her and that you want her to do for you.

In order to prepare her for what you are about to ask of her, you might want to show her a story in which a woman takes control of her husband the way you want her to do. The Internet is full of these kinds of stories. You should have no problem finding one to show her.

You could also write her a letter. Tell her how you feel and explain the benefits of such a relationship and how it could improve your marriage and even your family life. Explain that you would like her to be in charge of your sex-life and that you are willing to do whatever it takes to achieve it. Start doing some things to help her around the house. After all, if you are not willing to do them now, what makes you think you will enjoy doing them later, just because she tells you to?

First of all, you need to realize that, in an FLR, you are NOT the center, the focus, of the relationship. If you are going into it with the hopes of making your sex-life unbelievably fantastic, you have a rude awakening coming. In a true FLR, you (the sub) are going to be doing a great deal of work. Not all of it will be fun and games. You should realize that your focus must be on her and her happiness. Happiness does NOT necessarily mean more sex for you (or for her). Nor does it mean giving her all the sex she wants. It means, giving of yourself, unselfishly, completely, and without expectation of sexual reward. It is hard! So be sure that's what you want.

When you first start out, don't tell her that there is anything you don't like about your current relationship. That would be negative. You want to stay positive. That's why you made your lists. Tell her that you want to to improve your marriage and get back to the way things should be. You want to be more helpful, more thoughtful, more attentive to her needs, but that you can't do it all by yourself. You need her help.

When you suggest that she take charge, don't tell her you want her to take charge of everything. That can seem way too intimidating for her. It sounds like you are trying to unload all your burdens on her. She will, most likely, reject you out of hand if you do it that way. So be willing to take it slow. She will need your support and understanding. Remember, this is as new to her as it once was to you. You don't want to scare her away. You want to persuade her to give it a try.

Once you have made your case, give her some time to think about it. Don't push her into doing something she is not sure of. Give her this book. Or maybe send her to some web sites that include FLR stories. Be careful if you choose the latter, some of those stories might scare her off.

Once your wife has had time to think about it, sit down and discuss it in detail. You will need to have a clear understanding of exactly what will be expected of both of you, as far as the relationship goes. Don't expect too much from her, at first. Let her move at her own pace. If she wants to do more, take more control, then fine. But if she doesn't want exactly what you want, try to negotiate something in between. Come to an agreement. Perhaps, put it in writing. That way, you both understand the others boundaries and limitations. You can always make changes later when you are both more comfortable with the way things are going.

If your wife enjoys having control of your sex-life, she may be much more willing to take on other aspects of your relationship as well. Just give her the time she needs to get used to things and don't push her into anything for which she is not ready. And good luck!

Made in the USA
Lexington, KY
24 March 2014